Reactions from readers to
A Loss Misunderstood

"The book is ground zero truth. Very raw and deeply powerful. Anyone who reads it will be affected by it and will reassess their own thoughts and previous actions."

"I have been reduced to both tears and admiration for the author's personal courage in sharing."

"This book transported me back in time to when I had a medical procedure after my own miscarriage. I once again remembered the pain of the finality of that pregnancy. I found it healing to cry . . . even after 27 years!"

"This book is important because we all have a need to share our thoughts and feelings and to be understood. It takes a lot of courage to come face to face with the pain and fear in our lives, but it can be a huge part of the healing. I love how this book encourages the reader to journal and write their own story as the author shares hers."

"I look forward to when I can share *A Loss Misunderstood* with some special people in my life."

"This book is very emotionally powerful. It took me back to my dark days of curling up on the couch and crying for days. I think it truly is a situation that you can only understand if you've been through it. I've heard too many off-color comments from otherwise intelligent people to believe that they are in the minority. It's not their fault, they just don't get it."

"Thank you for sharing this. I shared it with my wife, and I know she'll feel glad that she's not the 'only one' going through this."

A Loss Misunderstood

Healing Your Grieving Heart
After Miscarriage

JACLYN PIERIS

CHANGING LIVES PRESS

Disclaimer: Please consult your physician for medical advice before beginning any procedure or dietary program, especially if you are currently taking any prescription or over-the-counter medications, are pregnant, are a minor, or have any type of medical condition.

The information contained in this book is designed to maintain good health and does not claim to treat or cure disease. It is not a substitute for regular medical care.

 CHANGING LIVES PRESS
P.O. Box 140189
Howard Beach, NY 11414
www.changinglivespress.com

Library of Congress Cataloging-in-Publication Data is available through the Library of Congress.

Edited by Lisa Espinoza

Cover and Interior design: Gary A. Rosenberg

Printed in the United States of America

10   9   8   7   6   5   4   3   2   1

Contents

"That maybe even if we're not always so glad to be here, it's our task to immerse ourselves anyway: wade straight through it, right through the cesspool, while keeping eyes and hearts open."

—THEODORE DECKER, *THE GOLDFINCH*
BY DONNA TARTT

Preface

To most young people, "growing up and starting a family" seems the most inevitable thing in the world. In our society, women (and men) often expect to be able to regulate their fertility until they feel ready to choose to become pregnant. Or so they think . . .

In so many ways, we are used to being able to control our future—where we go to college, our vocation and where we work, where we live, even our relationships. So when we are faced with the inability to control the process of a healthy pregnancy, the psychological implications can be devastating. Interactions with friends and family can become strained. Every TV program, magazine, and billboard poster portrays images of happy bouncing babies. People struggling to become pregnant can feel isolated, even paranoid. They begin to question—why me? What have I done wrong? Is it something I am eating or drinking, doing or not doing? They struggle to analyze why this is happening to them when it seems that all around them there are "undeserved" people getting pregnant so easily. There is a shame, an embarrassment about failing to achieve something that is regarded as so "natural."

As a specialist in Subfertility for many decades, these are recurring themes I hear from my patients on a daily basis, whatever their background, racial, or social group. There is a universal feeling of suffering and isolation by the time they finally reach a specialist. They cannot believe that this is happening to them. They feel they should have been able to get pregnant unaided and often have very mixed emotions about receiving treatment. They are grateful to receive the help necessary to have a child but at the same time are sometimes resentful about being in this situation at all.

One of the recurring complaints is how long it all takes. This, of course, is because women only ovulate once a month, and the oocyte only lives for 24 hours, so with the best will in the world, treatments can take months and sometimes years.

And of course, conceiving is only the start of a long and often stressful journey. Antenatal screening offers incredible opportunities to help avoid, or diagnose early, certain conditions, but miscarriage is the commonest complication of early pregnancy and is hard to predict or avoid. Joy is given and then taken away in such a cruel way.

Realizing that you are not alone can offer enormous support, as can talking with people having had a similar experience. Jaclyn's book gives an amazing insight into one person's, one couple's, one family's struggle with trying to start that elusive family, and I highly recommend her book to anyone in this situation.

Good luck to you all.

Dr Elizabeth Owen, MD, FRCOG
Consultant Obstetrician and Gynecologist
Lead for Subfertility

"The most beautiful people we have known are those who have known defeat, known suffering, known struggle, known loss, and have found their way out of the depths. These persons have an appreciation, a sensitivity, and an understanding of life that fills them with compassion, gentleness, and a deep loving concern. Beautiful people do not just happen."

—ELISABETH KUBLER-ROSS,
PSYCHIATRIST AND AUTHOR

Introduction

The pain and grief surrounding a woman's struggle to bring a healthy baby into this world is complex. Yet time and again I hear of women whose families and friends seem unable to grasp the pain and desperation that a woman carries until her healthy baby is born. "How long have you been trying to get pregnant?" "How far along were you when you miscarried?" These questions can leave women feeling as though the justification for their continued heartache is being assessed—as if a woman in her twenties who has been trying for years to have a baby shouldn't be as upset as a woman in her thirties because one has more "time" than the other.

Yes, along with a woman's physical battle to conceive or maintain a pregnancy come the incorrect assumptions made by others regarding how we should feel or react to our situation. There are the hurtful comments, and there is the obvious absence of comments. There are the guilt trips and the timelines placed upon our emotional healing. There are the numerous appointments with doctors, some of whom possess such poor bedside manner that their demeanor can leave us feeling broken for days. There are the ubiquitous strollers pushed by the brigades of moms who are bonding over their common denominator, the pregnancy announcements on social media sites, and the rosy-cheeked pregnant women with the impeccable timing who seem to wait for just the opportune moment to step out their doors into the paths of us, the childless, who are left wishing to melt into the pavement.

Perhaps even those closest to us want to minimize our sadness because it is too much for them to bear. Yet expecting women to compartmentalize their emotions and move through difficult feelings quickly is wishful thinking. Our bodies are not cooperating with a desired outcome that we had always assumed would be easily achieved. We can't rush through our feelings of isolation and guilt for continuing to love and long for the baby that we never even had. This kind of heartache cannot be manipulated to fit someone else's expectation for our process.

Every woman's journey to create a life is unique to her, struggle or not. It is my hope that my story will resonate with others who are feeling alone or misunderstood during their attempts to give birth to a healthy baby. I also hope that this book can be passed on to friends and family who want to better understand the feelings that women and their partners can experience when trying to start a family.

I encourage you to grab a pen, crayon, or marker and begin writing down your thoughts and emotions on the lined pages throughout the book, releasing them from your mind. Let this book help carry the weight of your emotions.

"Oh God!
I'm so mad I don't know what to do!
Oh God, I want to know why!
Why?!
Lord, I wish I could understand . . .
I don't think I can take this!
I don't think I can take this!
I just want to hit somebody until they feel
as bad as I do! I just want to hit something!
I want to hit it hard!"

—SALLY FIELD AS MALYNNE,
STEEL MAGNOLIAS

CHAPTER 1

And So It Begins

They say that knowledge is power, that with a solid education, our lives will be easier. All of the information we learned in our many years of math, science, and history classes should have prepared us for our future as adults, living and working in the real world . . . right?

Right now, I feel as though the education system has FAILED me. Should we not have been given advice and information on how to handle THIS?

No one ever mentioned that even the strongest of marriages could struggle to stand up against THIS.

I don't remember being taught that "when" to have children and 'how many' children to have is not actually up to me but in the hands of Mother Nature.

In my grief, I find myself crying and updating my status on Facebook as tears fall on the keys of my laptop. "I will be closing my Facebook account tomorrow. If you'd like to keep in touch, you can email me at the following personal email account . . . "

What I really want to write on this social media site, where the details of our lives play out publically day by day, is that my heart has been torn in little pieces one post at a time. I want to say, "How dare all of you post pictures of your pregnancy scans and the numerous images of you posing with your hands holding your dress tightly under your bump for everyone to see the exact outline of your protruding belly. Do we all need to be a part of every change your body is making over the next nine months?! Why can't you be humble and let *your* joy be *your* joy?" Ugh.

I drop my head, exhausted by my anger and the acuteness of my loss. My emptiness. My envy.

I stop myself from posting what's really on my mind. At least I have just enough self-awareness to know that I am being irrational, that I too would be posting the same pictures and status updates if I were pregnant or had a beautiful new-born baby to show off.

My husband walks into the room and asks me if I'm okay. My fury reignites, and I start shouting at him. I am blaming him for my misery. As I spit out a string of words that barely make sense, I know that I am misplacing my anger. But in this moment, I feel desperate to rid myself of this pulsing negative energy that is raging inside of me. I need to pick a fight with someone who can yell back, and until my ovaries learn to speak, I continue to hurt my husband.

Guilt.

He never reciprocates, and my mind is screaming, "Yell back! Yell back!" He watches me with sad eyes, and I so badly want him to put me in my place. I want to see his anger instead of the sadness that is draining the life from his eyes. As always, he refrains. Anger is surging from my core and out to the ends of my extremities. I feel myself looking for an object to throw or a door to slam.

I could wreak havoc on this house. I could break windows. I could punch my fist through our bedroom mirror.

Something inside is holding me back from unleashing this fury that is boiling inside of me.

I tell my husband that we should have started trying earlier. I can't even say the word "baby" out loud. That might normalize the situation, and for me, a woman who can't produce life, the situation is anything but normal. I remind my husband that I wanted to start trying a year earlier, but we waited because *he* wasn't quite ready. I tell him that we'd have a baby by now if we had started when *I* was ready.

I can't stand him looking at me anymore, so I storm into the bathroom and slam the door shut behind me. I look into the mirror at my tear-stained face and swollen eyes. I look ugly on the outside, and I feel even uglier on the inside.

I hate what I see.

The tears begin to flow again, and I cover my face with my hands.

Ugh. Ugly crier.

How much more can I take? How many other people will announce their pregnancies and deliver their first and second babies before I fall pregnant again? How many times will I have to act happy for others, when really, all I feel is pure envy?

How many more times will I have to listen to people tell me, "It'll be okay. It will happen for you. One day you'll look back on this and laugh." I sure as hell can't wait for that day, and unless you can tell me when "it" will happen, those words of encouragement mean nothing to me.

And so my grief begins.

"To love means to be actively concerned for the life and the growth of another."

—IRVIN D. YALOM,
PSYCHOTHERAPIST AND AUTHOR

CHAPTER 2

Let's Start a Family

Throughout my twenties, I was overwhelmed by the idea of growing and then pushing a baby out of a relatively small opening of my body. The stories of labor gone wrong horrified me and left me so uncertain about the birthing process that even the birthing scene from the movie *Knocked Up* left me in tears.

But as with so many things, time seemed to chip away at my fears. As I was nearing my 30th birthday, I woke up one morning and decided to stop taking my birth control and start trying to get pregnant—it was time. Worries that my irregular menstrual cycle would make it incredibly hard to determine when I was ovulating were unfounded. Two months after deciding to "try," I took a pregnancy test and was shocked to see a positive result.

I was stunned at what, at the time, seemed like amazing luck. When we saw the positive pregnancy test, both my husband and I were immediately cautious, afraid to believe that having a baby could actually be this easy. Let's just say, we react more intensely when we find a Cadbury Cream Egg lodged at the back of our silverware drawer than we did upon seeing the positive test. There was no jumping into each other's arms and no tears of joy. Perhaps we knew deep down inside that, despite our healthy lifestyles, we weren't going to be among the lucky ones.

My husband and I were aware that if something were going to go wrong, it would most likely happen within the first trimester (three months). We followed the rule of thumb that everyone had passed down to us and refrained from spreading the word until we had our first scan.

About two weeks before my first scan, which took place at 14 weeks, I suddenly had a feeling of emptiness in my abdomen. Up until that point, I had felt full and bloated. I noticed this new sensation while walking home from a stroll in the park with my husband. I tried to push it out of my mind, thinking that if there were something wrong, I'd bleed. But there was no blood.

About one week before my scan, I was at the gym lying on a mat doing ab exercises when I felt a slight burning sensation on the right-hand side of my uterus. I immediately stopped what I was doing, pulled myself upright, and felt fear wash over me.

Something was not right.

IN MY WORDS

This is when I realized I wanted to be a mom . . .

_____

_____

_____

_____

_____

To me, parenthood is . . .

_____

_____

_____

_____

_____

My partner and I decided to start trying for
a family when . . .

_____

_____

_____

_____

_____

_____

This is when we realized that starting a family would be a challenge . . .

_____

_____

_____

_____

_____

The doctors we have worked with have been . . .

_____

_____

_____

_____

_____

Our family's and friends' reactions to our situation have been . . .

_____

_____

_____

_____

_____

"When do you think you lost your faith?"

"I remember the exact moment. I was on the phone with my mother and she was trying to counsel me through this thing. And when nothing she was saying was making me feel any better she said, 'Bethany, God has a plan.'

"I was so angry with her. I was like, 'What about my plan? Ya know? I had planned to have a family with my husband. Wasn't that plan good enough for God?' Apparently not."

—BEN AFFLECK AND LINDA FIORENTINO
IN THE MOVIE DOGMA (1999)

CHAPTER 3

An Unviable Pregnancy

On the morning of my scan, I went to work as usual. I remember wondering why I didn't feel more excited about the afternoon's appointment. I was going to see a picture of my baby for the very first time, and then finally this would all seem real. I tried to give myself a pep talk, but there remained a numbness inside.

I was working at an institution of higher education at that time, and my department had planned to go out to lunch together before the start of a new academic year. I knew I'd have to miss the gathering for my scan, and at the end of our department meeting, I decided to announce my pregnancy to everyone. All five females jumped from their chairs and gave me warm hugs and showed genuine happiness for me. The experience of being congratulated on my pregnancy seemed surreal, and I felt as though I was some sort of fake, deceiving people with my story.

After the meeting, I sat in my office and anxiously waited for my husband to arrive so that we could drive to the hospital. I chugged my required liter of water, smiling at people as they walked by my office, despite the worry that lingered in my mind.

When my husband and I arrived at the hospital, I sat in the waiting room impatiently as I watched 15 minutes slowly tick by on the clock. The pressure from my full bladder began to bring quite a bit of discomfort. After what seemed like an eternity, my husband and I were invited by the scan technician back to a white, sterile room, and I limped along, my bladder ready to burst. I took off my trousers and eased myself up onto the padded table and lifted my shirt. The room was cold, and the technician looked tired. The lady scanned my lower abdomen, and I held my breath, desperate to see a tiny outline of my baby come to life on screen.

Something wasn't right.

The room was silent.

Nothing.

"You know, you can often miss a period when you first come off of birth control. Are you sure you're pregnant?" said the lady.

"Yes," I told her, exasperated that she would think I could make such a mistake. "I took five pregnancy tests, and they all came out positive, along with having tender breasts, exhaustion, and a bloated abdomen." I reeled off my symptoms as proof in one quick breath. But then, after a minute, I began to question myself. Could I have read all five of the pregnancy tests wrong?

The technician seemed perplexed and told me to walk to the toilet and fully empty my bladder as she wanted to conduct an internal scan. I walked out into the hallway towards the toilet in a daze, not allowing myself to fully comprehend what was happening.

Don't let your mind go there yet.

Self-preservation.

When I came back into the room and repositioned myself onto the bed, the technician held a wand that looked to be 12 inches long. She rubbed some lubricant onto the tip and then down under the sheet it went. Could this situation be any more personal, both emotionally and physically?

Then came the explanation: An empty pregnancy sac was found. It appeared that development had ceased around six weeks. The technician patted my back and let out a few sighs to let me know how sorry she felt for us. I began to cry as my husband picked up my trousers and underwear off of the floor and started to help me get dressed. We were ushered out of the room and on to the Early Pregnancy Unit that was located in another building on the hospital's campus.

The scan that I had been anxiously awaiting for three months was over. The day that I had counted down to, crossing off each little square in my calendar, was supposed to be one of the best days of my life. If only I had known that I was actually getting closer and closer to one of the worst days of my life. Every minute that passed brought further realization of the situation, and the pain of the loss began to settle into my bones where it would stay for a very long time.

My earlier worries had been confirmed. As we made our way to the Early Pregnancy Unit, we passed people who seemed to look at us with curiosity, wondering about the source of our distress. When we finally made it to the waiting area, we thankfully were not left on our own for long. The young female doctor welcomed us into her office and began to explain what was to happen next. I clearly remember the kindness in her voice and demeanor—not to be underestimated during such a time of distress.

We would have to have another scan in one week to ensure that growth in the womb had indeed stopped. From that point, my options would be to wait and allow my body to miscarry naturally, to take a pill to induce labor, or to undergo a procedure whereby I'd be put under by anesthesia and would have the pregnancy sac and everything else that had begun to grow inside of me removed. Without hesitation, I opted for the surgery. I did not want to experience labor pains or wait around for my body to begin to expel that which should have been.

The following week in between appointments was torture. My body still believed that it was pregnant, so I continued to have sore breasts and exhaustion, and my abdomen was bloated. If this was an "unviable" pregnancy, I did not want to feel like I was pregnant. But I did, and it felt cruel.

Seven more days of feeling like I was pregnant, yet knowing that my time as a mother was over.

IN MY WORDS

Not being able to get pregnant, facing a miscarriage, or seeing a negative pregnancy test leaves me feeling this way emotionally . . .

_____

_____

_____

_____

_____

_____

_____

_____

Physically, my body feels . . .

_____

_____

_____

_____

_____

_____

_____

_____

This is how my partner and I have reacted
to our situation . . .

_____

_____

_____

_____

_____

_____

_____

_____

_____

*"People are like stained glass windows.
They sparkle and shine when the sun is out,
but when the darkness sets in,
their true beauty is revealed
only if there is a light from within."*

—ELISABETH KUBLER-ROSS,
PSYCHIATRIST AND AUTHOR

CHAPTER 4

Facing an Ending

After our long morning at the hospital, my husband and I headed to the parking lot to make our way home. We suddenly remembered that his parents were waiting at our flat to celebrate with us post-scan. They happened to be in the area and had decided to stop in to see us on what was supposed to be a momentous occasion: the first grandbaby in the family.

I slid myself into the front seat of the car while my husband stood outside in the cold to call his parents and warn them that all had not gone well. We drove home in virtual silence, neither of us knowing what to say, unable to comprehend that after three months of feeling like parents, we were . . . nothing.

When we pulled into our driveway, I didn't want to go inside the flat. I didn't want to see the sadness and confusion in my in-laws' eyes. I certainly didn't want to repeat and relive the morning. On the contrary, I wanted to jump on a plane and head somewhere far, far away—and fast. So this is the fight-or-flight reaction that we learned about in high school psychology class.

When we entered the flat, my in-laws stayed in our kitchen and waited for us to come to them. After I took off my shoes and put down my bag, I slowly walked in their direction. I could see a vase of fresh flowers that they had tried to hide from view. Nope, there was nothing to congratulate us on anymore. They hugged us, and I could see that my mother-in-law had been crying.

We made our way into the living room, sat down on the couch, and began to explain what had taken place at the hospital. I remember looking out our large glass window at the grey sky. Everything around me looked depressing. I tuned into what my husband was saying to his parents, and they looked stunned and began to search for the right words. But of course, there was nothing anyone could say to bring comfort.

Following an interminable week of waiting, the

ERPC (Evacuation of Retained Products of Conception) procedure went as well as it could have gone. Despite being seen in the day surgery unit where people are in and out all day long, the empathy I was shown was overwhelming. The doctor who was to conduct the procedure, along with the anesthesiologist, came to speak to me before I was wheeled into the operating room. They greeted me by shaking my hand and placing their hands on my shoulders as a way, it seemed, to pass on their sympathy. How refreshing that the doctors and nurses didn't avoid or shy away from acknowledging the situation that brought me to them.

I was wheeled into the operating room with blankets tightly tucked underneath my legs and back to keep me warm and feeling secure. There was a team of five waiting for me under bright lights in the middle of the operating room. Moments later, I was put under. This was the end of my pregnancy.

When I was back in the recovery room, my husband was brought back to my bedside. When the nurse pulled back the curtain and we made eye contact, I saw the look of pity in his eyes. He was dealing with a deep sadness that he had already begun to bury inside. He began to ask me questions but quickly realized that I couldn't speak. Each time I tried, tears would follow.

Later that day, back at the flat, as I lay in my bed curled under a thick duvet trying to hide from the cruel world, my mind began to wander to thoughts of what had taken place in the operating room: *Who untucked the blanket and pulled up my gown? How exposed was I to everyone in the room? How much was vacuumed out of me?* I'm not sure why I began to picture or imagine what transpired in that room. Perhaps I needed to understand exactly what had happened during those moments where motherhood had been physically taken away from me in order for me to gain a tiny piece of closure.

IN MY WORDS

This is how I generally feel about endings . . .

_____

_____

_____

_____

_____

Typically, this is how I have handled endings
in my life . . .

_____

_____

_____

_____

_____

_____

This is how my partner handles endings . . .

_____

_____

_____

_____

_____

_____

"I was in love with the sound of the slamming door, it sounded the way I felt, like Damn you to hell! And I hate what you're doing to me! And Life sucks."

ELLEN WITTLINGER, AUTHOR

CHAPTER 5

When Will
I Feel Better?

The miscarriage happened leading up to my busiest week of the entire year at work. It was New Student Orientation Week at the university, and on top of the sadness I was feeling due to our loss, I felt guilty for not being in attendance to oversee this huge event. Despite the guilt, I knew that I could not have functioned at work. At the same time, being at home alone with my thoughts wasn't working out very well either.

Immediately after the surgery, I began setting timelines for myself. *In two weeks, I will feel better.*

Over and over, two weeks would roll around, and I wouldn't feel any better—sometimes I even felt worse. At the end of each and every self-imposed timeline, I was left devastated, feeling no better than I had in the weeks before.

I spoke to my parents almost every day, and without fail I'd end up crying. I wasn't in control of my emotions, and I wondered what they were thinking on the other end of the phone. What I did know was that I needed to be allowed to feel sorry for myself, and for my family to accept that I was going to act irrationally for a while.

Two weeks after the surgery, I was still bleeding and tired of wearing giant maxi pads that left me feeling dirty. This was yet another daily reminder of what my husband and I had lost. At the same time, we received a phone call that would inflamed my emotions.

I was sitting in the room when my husband answered the phone. I knew the information that had been revealed from my husband's forced response. It was his sister calling to tell us she was pregnant. The family's first grandchild.

My husband tried to sound genuine in his excitement, but I could tell that his mind was reeling. I stood up and quickly walked myself to our bedroom, lay down on the bed, and cried.

Over those past several years since my husband and I were married, my in-laws had been regularly dropping hints that they wanted to become grandparents as soon as possible. Although my husband is the younger sibling, we were married first, and it seemed natural that we would be the first to start a family. Now their daughter would be fulfilling this yearning for them. Thoughts of family gatherings filled my head. I couldn't imagine how I would manage to watch my sister-in-law go through her pregnancy as it developed, knowing that I should be experiencing the very same thing. It felt like God was playing some sort of cruel joke and had plucked away my pregnancy and handed it to her. I imagined her and my in-laws' excitement in the face of our misery.

Of all times that my sister-in-law could have fallen pregnant. She had only been married for three months, and to top it off, she and her husband hadn't even been trying to get pregnant. They had planned on waiting another year. I just could not comprehend how life could be so unfair in the way it took life from one person and handed it to another.

And so my grief continued.

MY STORY

I must avoid these people or things (e.g. social media sites, TV shows, advertisements, etc.) in order to stay afloat . . .

_____

_____

_____

_____

_____

_____

_____

These are the people or things that I count on for support . . .

_____

_____

_____

_____

_____

_____

_____

This is a short description of the loss and grief
that I have experienced previously in my life . . .

_____

_____

_____

_____

_____

_____

_____

_____

_____

"The only time you should ever look back,
is to see how far you've come."

—Unknown

CHAPTER 6

My Life in Numbers

I had one miscarriage after three months of thinking I was a mom.

One week after my first scan, I had a procedure to remove all remnants of motherhood from my body.

Two weeks after the miscarriage, my sister-in-law phoned to tell us that she was pregnant with her first baby—and they hadn't even been trying to get pregnant.

I bled for three weeks after the ERPC.

I went to see a counselor two months after my first miscarriage.

It took four months for me to regain a minuscule amount of positivity after the first unviable pregnancy.

I was only allowed two counseling sessions through the National Health Service (NHS)* since I miscarried before 14 weeks.

One year after my first miscarriage, I conceived for a second time.

Four weeks after I conceived, I had a second miscarriage.

The NHS won't assist me in my struggle to conceive and maintain a pregnancy until I've tried to conceive naturally for two years.

I've seen seven different doctors regarding my pregnancy struggles, and only three had an adequate bedside manner.

Eight of my friends have conceived since my first miscarriage.

One out of every hundred couples will have recurrent miscarriages (three or more).

Numbers are rolling around in my head. Everywhere I go, I'm being presented with timelines and medical statistics, and I feel exhausted by them.

---

*The National Health Service (NHS), implemented in 1948, is the publicly funded health care system in the United Kingdom. The system is primarily funded through central taxation and National Insurance or contributions paid by employers and employees towards the cost of select state benefits. Most services are free of charge to legal residents of the UK.

I have considered throwing away my calendar, but I have to track my cycles and try to determine when I'm ovulating. I want to let go but I can't. I can't chance missing an opportunity to conceive. I wish someone else could take over for me. I don't want to be in charge of planning anymore.

IN MY WORDS

This has been our timeline to date with regard to our journey to produce a healthy baby . . .

_____

_____

_____

_____

_____

_____

_____

This is how long I'll continue to try to become pregnant and maintain a healthy pregnancy . . .

_____

_____

_____

"Consciously or not, we are all on a quest for answers, trying to learn the lessons of life. We grapple with fear and guilt. We search for meaning, love, and power. We try to understand fear, loss, and time. We seek to discover who we are and how we can become truly happy."

—ELISABETH KUBLER-ROSS,
PSYCHIATRIST AND AUTHOR

CHAPTER 7

Grasping for Time

After my first miscarriage, all I could think of were numbers. I thought of the number of months it took me to get pregnant and the number of weeks that I thought I was pregnant, when in reality, all growth had ceased. I thought of the number of months until we'd be able to try to get pregnant again and the minimum number of months until I'd have a baby if I could conceive right away.

The little black Moleskine calendar that I had always carried in my bag to keep my life organized became my enemy, yet I couldn't let it go. I crossed each day off meticulously, trying to grasp control of time, yet knowing full well that I was at its mercy.

For months, numbers continued rolling around in my head. The doctors continued to give me advice such as, "If you feel ready emotionally, you can start trying to conceive again in three months." They said it as if they were giving me joyful news that would lift my spirits. "Yes, that's right . . . you can try in just three months!" They didn't understand—three months seemed like a lifetime to wait and left me feeling deflated.

From the day I found out that I was pregnant, I had the next 365 days of my life planned. I knew when I'd fly home to the U.S. for a baby shower to celebrate with my nearest and dearest. I knew the day and month that I'd need to cancel my gym membership in preparation for being heavily pregnant and unable to work out. I had figured out how much money we needed to save to cover all of our bills during my maternity leave.

I had Googled my way through baby website after baby website looking at strollers that were suitable for my daily jogs and browsing diaper bags that would suit a man so that my husband would be a stylish dad while on baby duty. I began spending time every evening looking at Pottery Barn's website for ideas on how to decorate the baby's room. I knew it was too early to begin buying any supplies, but I couldn't help but let my mind wander and imagine how life was going to change.

After the miscarriage, I became hyperaware of my age and how old I'd be when I might finally have a baby. I compared myself to girls I had gone to high school with, most of whom had two or three kids at this point. I felt like I was being left behind in the dust.

I began gauging how many "good" years I thought I'd have left in life. To me, the good years were this time when I still felt full of energy and was still mistaken for one of the students at my place of work. But how much longer would this last? How long would I have to spend feeling sad, my thoughts consumed with this longing for parenthood? How many of my best years would be wasted wallowing in sadness?

Now in my thirties, I was nearing the age when a woman's fertility is drastically reduced. News stories warning women of the dangers of starting a family past the age of 35 became permanently etched in my mind, and I felt a sense of panic.

I started thinking about death and how much I would, or would not, be able to accomplish in the good years I had left. *If and when I finally have a baby, am I going to be an "old" mom? If*

I can't have children, what will become my focus in life? Will I become sickeningly dedicated to my career? Shopping, reading, and all of the other pastimes that normally gave me pleasure began to seem pointless. *What is the point in life anymore? What is my purpose if I can't have a family? Will my relationship with my husband last if we remain childless?*

Somehow I was going to have to learn to let go of this ever-present fear of time leaving me in its wake, but I had no idea how.

MY STORY

Time seems to be moving . . .

_____

_____

_____

_____

_____

These are my feelings around the timings that are
attached to this process . . .

_____

_____

_____

_____

_____

_____

_____

_____

_____

_____

_____

*"The opinion which other people have
of you is their problem, not yours."*

—ELISABETH KUBLER-ROSS,
PSYCHIATRIST AND AUTHOR

CHAPTER 8

The Things People Say...

And then there were the comments of others who had a need to provide me with advice or to try to figure out how the miscarriage occurred.

"Did the doctor say what you need to do differently next time?"

"Had you toned down your workouts?"

"Were you taking prenatal vitamins?"

"It WILL happen for you! You'll just have to be patient."

"You must enjoy this time you have alone

together. One day you'll have kids and you'll long for the peace and quiet that you have now."

"It's in God's plan, and one day you'll realize why this has happened."

"Don't ask, 'Why me?' Ask, 'Why not me?'"

"You'll just HAVE to act happy when other people announce their pregnancy news to you."

"Do you want us to return the stroller that we had bought for you?"

"Have you considered adoption?"

"This couldn't be the most upsetting thing that's happened to you. It is? Wow, you've had it easy."

"I don't have any time to clean the house since the baby arrived. You're lucky you have so much time on your hands."

"Why can't you spend more time around our baby? You know, you could be a really good aunt if you wanted to be."

"When do you think you'll feel better? I mean, what if you have a third miscarriage—then what?"

I've always been a sensitive person and have regularly let people's negative comments hold me down. It's something that I've been working on since I entered adulthood, as I've spent way too much time feeling disappointed by others' actions. The words or actions tend to stay in my mind on playback, as if on a never-ending loop. I always thought that if I could just understand or know the motive behind the person's comment, then perhaps I could move on. And under these circumstances, my thought process was the same: "How could they not know that their words could be so hurtful?"

I'd say to my husband, "Do you really have to go through a miscarriage yourself to have a modicum amount of sensitivity for people in our situation?" I felt angry and resentful; dealing with the comments of others was a hindrance in helping me to work through my grief. How could I take the time to recognize and understand my own emotions if I was always trying to work through everyone else's?

In the end, I decided to write down every comment that upset me (of course, I was easily able to pull all of them from memory!), and even though I didn't forget about them completely, I found somewhere to park these thoughts instead of allowing them to continue racing around in my mind.

In time, I was also able to speak with some of the people who had said truly hurtful things to me. Every time, the person remembered the exchange and was either genuinely surprised that the comment was so upsetting or was immediately able to acknowledge their mistake. A couple of people admitted that they had snapped at me because they were in some way triggered by my situation, and their defense mechanism was to minimize the significance of what I was going through. And just as I had thought, as soon as I understood why they had made the hurtful comment, I was able to take another step away from the pain.

My Story

These are the comments that people have made that have upset me . . .

_____

_____

_____

_____

_____

_____

These are the comments that people have made that have comforted me . . .

This is how I react and cope with the comments (both hurtful and comforting) made by others . . .

---

*"I'll have the worst day of my life,
with a side of guilt, please!"*

—JIM CARREY IN *BRUCE ALMIGHTY* (2003)

CHAPTER 9

And the E-mails People Write . . .

It was the summer after my first miscarriage, and it had been almost exactly one year since I had lost the pregnancy. Our disappointment at not being able to conceive after so long was heartbreaking. Needless to say, it had been a tough year, and we had counted down the days until we'd be visiting my family in the States. We would spend one week in California with my younger brother and his girlfriend, followed by a week in Pennsylvania with my older brother, his wife, and their two little boys.

When we arrived in Pennsylvania to visit my sister-in-law's family, I immediately began picking up clues that something was up. Normally a devout wine drinker, my sister-in-law poured herself a large glass of red and then let it sit untouched for the rest of the evening. I noticed that my brother was speaking to her in a gentler-than-normal tone of voice, and he was more tactile and affectionate. The final clue was discovered when I happened to walk by the kitchen counter as my sister-in-law's phone was ringing, and I looked down to see the word "OB/GYN" pop up across the screen. My sister-in-law was pregnant with their third baby.

My heart sank.

To see a couple's excitement and renewed devotion to one another when they know that they are creating a new life is bittersweet for those of us who are reproductively challenged. I wanted to feel that love. I wanted to be able to spend nine months daydreaming of what our life was about to become.

And so, as our week progressed, I felt myself withdrawing into myself. The family moments that I should have been enjoying and savoring were tarnished by my profound sadness and desperation for a baby.

About a week after I returned to the UK, I

received a phone call from our friends in Australia who wanted to share the exciting news that they were expecting their first baby. Within minutes, I also received an email from a family member expressing their disappointment about the negative feelings that I had "directed" toward my brother and his wife. I didn't understand. How could my choice to suffer in silence be so hurtful to my family? I could have expressed my emotions verbally, but that most certainly would have made for an awkward, negative situation. So, despite my efforts to handle my struggle in the best way I knew how, I had affected others in a negative way.

The email sent me into a rage, and I called my mother yelling, "What do any of you have to be upset about?! I'm doing the best that I can, and I'm sorry if my grief is inconveniencing you! I'm sorry a celebration couldn't be held to announce the birth of their THIRD baby!" My mother stayed calm and suggested that I look at the situation from the family's perspective. I didn't get it. I wasn't verbally abusive, and I didn't stay hidden in bed under my covers all day. How was my behavior so offensive? I hung up the phone and threw it across the room.

About six months later, I received an email from someone on my husband's side of the family telling me that my husband and I were being hurtful by not seeing his sister's baby more. The email stemmed from an invitation to the "Baby's First Christmas Party" that would include numerous family members and friends. I declined the invitation, feeling as though I could handle smaller gatherings for the baby, but not this kind of event where I imagined there would be large groups of people huddled around the baby oohing and ahhing. I lived in fear of getting myself into situations where aunts and uncles would approach me and say, "You've been married for quite a few years already. When will you start trying for a baby?" I just couldn't face one more jab to the heart.

The email felt scolding and told me that my husband and I could play a very important role in the baby's life if we chose to see him more often and that our decision to keep our distance was hurting the family. We were then instructed to have a discussion with one another about our behavior. Needless to say, I was once again enraged by what I perceived as our family's lack of empathy. My sister-in-law had announced her pregnancy two weeks after I miscarried and had a baby that was the same age as my baby should have been. I felt that I was being scolded for my grief.

At a time when we needed support from our family the most, we felt furthest from them. I was exhausted by my situation in life, and I had no energy to begin putting on some sort of an act. Staying away from babies (as much as was humanly possible) was the one way that I was able to stay afloat during our trying times. My husband and I decided that we would have to accept that others might feel hurt or offended but that we'd continue to do what we felt necessary in order to avoid further pain. If that meant missing a few birthday parties or other family gatherings, then that is what we would have to do.

MY STORY

These are the gatherings I've had to avoid,
or those that I was able to attend . . .

_____

_____

_____

_____

_____

_____

_____

This is how our family or friends have reacted
when we have declined invitations . . .

_____

_____

_____

_____

_____

_____

_____

_____

When we're in mixed company, these are
the questions that I try to avoid being asked,
or that hurt the most . . .

_____

_____

_____

_____

_____

_____

_____

_____

_____

*"So God is picking on you.
Is that what you're saying?"*

"No! He's ignoring me completely!"

—JENNIFER ANISTON AND JIM CAREY
IN *BRUCE ALMIGHTY* (2003)

CHAPTER 10

Mom? Dad? Help!

After the miscarriage, I realized that this was the first time that I couldn't call my parents for help. I was living in England, and they were in the U.S., so there was only so much they could do to reach out and try to make me feel better. That made me angry.

I had never felt so out of control, and control was important to me. I was the young woman who successfully took charge of planning my future with my husband. I was the one who had wanted to move to England after we finished graduate school. I was the one who decided that we'd move to the outskirts of London. I was the one who found us our first flat together. I was the one who had decided that I wanted to start a family at the age of 30. Little did I know, that was one choice that I had no control over. Mother Nature would decide when we'd have a baby—and I hated her for it.

And so I found myself behaving like a child. Perhaps if I cried long enough or cried hard enough, someone would come to my rescue and alleviate my pain. But once again, I would come to realize that my thoughts were completely irrational, and I'd have to continue playing the waiting game, like it or not.

In turn, my parents felt pained knowing that there wasn't anything they could do for me. They too felt their excitement at the prospect of having another grandchild taken away. My mother found support through daring to discuss my situation with others. I think this takes guts, as you never know how others will react to your pain, and their apathy can leave you reeling and wondering why you ever tried to reach out in the first place. Luckily, time after time, she discovered that someone close to her had experienced one or more miscarriages, too. The pain my mother saw in many women's eyes as she would share her story of loss was testament that years or even decades after a miscarriage, the thought of the loss still cuts deeply.

As for my father, to my surprise, he was my staunch supporter. He never tried to give me advice, but instead gave me his undivided attention when I needed to ramble on in circles. Normally a no-nonsense kind of man, he allowed me to go a little crazy, and to feel comfortable as I cried and blew my nose loudly into the telephone receiver. He never asked me to consider the "other side" of a situation when I'd tell him of family members' emails that left me feeling less than supported. He never scolded me when every word out of my mouth was pessimistic. My father was somehow able to support me better than other women in my life, not only because of his ability to withhold advice, but also because of his calming presence that I was able to feel over the phone. Living an ocean away from one another was tough. But when we were together, his non-verbal communication showed me boundless love and support.

Sometimes it's a look, a touch, or even silence that can begin to put the world to right.

My Story . . .

This person is our staunch supporter . . .

_____

_____

_____

If I had to pick four emotions to best describe
how I feel/have felt through our journey to start
a family, I'd use the following words . . .

1. _____

2. _____

3. _____

4. _____

These are the moments that I have felt some calm,
or when I feel at peace with the world . . .

_____

_____

_____

_____

_____

_____

_____

*"Men usually must be taught to experience
and share (rather than to suppress
and evade) their sadness."*

—Irvin D. Yalom,
Psychotherapist and Author

CHAPTER 11

Remember the Boys

When writing my journal, I would frequently read through each section with my husband. This was a painful, yet therapeutic exercise for us both. Hot tears would well up behind my eyes, and I would bite my lower lip, trying my hardest to verbalize our situation without crying.

One evening, after I had read my latest entry to my husband, he looked at me and said, "Don't forget about the boys." His comment catapulted me back in time to the day I found out that my pregnancy was unviable. I was on the phone sobbing to my mom, and I remember that, right before we got off of the phone, she said to me,

"Don't forget about Paul. He, too, is in pain right now."

Our partners may not call their mothers and have a good cry or throw themselves into bed and hide under the duvet, but that does not mean that they aren't feeling the loss of a pregnancy. From personal experience, my husband threw his emotions to one side and focused all of his energy on taking care of me in my time of need. He began taking me to and picking me up from work every day so that I wouldn't have to take public transportation, which in itself can often be a stress-inducing experience. He cooked every meal and massaged my feet every night. He sent me text messages throughout the day letting me know that I was in his thoughts.

But no one can ignore or avoid their pain forever. About three months after the miscarriage, my husband fell apart. He came down with a cold that led to a chest infection he just couldn't kick. After finally admitting defeat, he decided to see a doctor. He was immediately asked if he was experiencing a high level of stress in his life, likely the primary contributing factor to his weakened immune system.

And then it clicked.

My husband realized that he wasn't faring as well as he was trying to lead himself to believe and that he needed to start the process of acknowledging and working through his grief. He slowly started to discuss his feelings with me, and I urged him to communicate regularly with his family. I wanted him to make sure they were aware that it was not only my world that had been rocked since the miscarriages, but that he too was deeply wounded.

It wasn't easy for me to hear him discuss his emotions. It was a much more comfortable space having him act as my protector and caretaker than to witness his vulnerabilities which led to further awareness of my own. At the same time, it was a relief to know that I wasn't alone in my sadness. I had begun to wonder if something was wrong with me for feeling so upset.

Rather than healing our wounds, as the saying goes, it seemed that time simply brought more emerging emotions. My husband began to feel guilty that I had to bear the brunt of the physical effects of miscarrying. I went through the surgery, the internal scans, the blood work, the cramping, the daily peeing on ovulation test sticks, and the monthly pregnancy tests which always led to deep disappointment as we continued to try for a baby. My husband desperately wanted to be involved more, but there wasn't much for him to do other than to submit a sperm sample to ensure his physical health, and to have sex with me when we felt the time was right. Let's just say that his physical role in all of this seemed to involve more pleasure than not, and he felt guilty.

I needed to do whatever I could to help alleviate his feelings of guilt. The fact that he could not take an equal role in all of this was not his fault. It's just the way Mother Nature intended, whether I thought it was fair or not. We sat down and discussed ways for him to become more involved that would take some of the pressure off of me. As part of our plan, we went to the doctor's office and signed a letter of consent allowing my husband to obtain information on my behalf, whether it be to follow up on blood test results or to reschedule an appointment. This simple plan of action provided us both with a feeling of relief in that we could share more of the responsibilities in our quest to have a healthy pregnancy.

During those early days, I remember hearing my husband on the phone with family or friends and counting the seconds before I would hear them ask, "How's Jaclyn doing?" I rarely heard anyone ask my husband how he was coping. Later, he told me that people's lack of inquiring into his feelings allowed him to avoid his grief and continue to focus on me. Eventually, I told my husband about my mother's reminder to me, to never forget his pain. As soon as the words left my mouth, he was in tears.

Sometimes the first step to confronting our grief is to have another acknowledge it first. This can open the door for us to begin the journey to recovery. So, remember the boys. They are hurting, too.

MY STORY

This is how my partner has handled our situation . . .

_____

_____

_____

_____

_____

_____

_____

_____

This is how we try to support each other . . .

_____

_____

_____

_____

_____

_____

_____

_____

This is how others have/have not supported
my partner . . .

_____

_____

_____

_____

_____

_____

_____

_____

If I could go back in time to handle things
differently, I might . . .

_____

_____

_____

_____

_____

_____

_____

_____

*"Sometimes the smallest things
take up the most room in your heart."*
—WINNIE THE POOH

CHAPTER 12

Talk Therapy

As I was free-falling through the stages of grief, it became clear that I needed to see a counselor so that I could talk through my emotions with a professional. I needed to find someone who would show me unconditional positive regard and who could, ideally, empathize with my story. My husband called our hospital's Early Pregnancy Unit to find a contact. The hospital subsequently scheduled me to meet with one of their members of staff the very next day. That was by far the quickest we had ever been able to obtain an appointment through the National Health Service. My husband must have sounded desperate.

We were the counselor's last clients to be seen that day. When the woman called us back to her room from the waiting area, she looked tired and emotionless. I immediately wanted to turn and run for the door. I couldn't be around yet another person who could not connect with our pain.

The counselor opened our session by using silence as a technique to encourage us to begin the conversation. Having a background in counseling, and hence recognizing this technique, I became stubborn and remained silent. Our faces mirrored hers—worn and weary. Finally, the counselor broke the silence and asked us what had brought us in to see her.

As soon as I opened my mouth, the emotions that I had been trying to suppress began bubbling up to the surface and overflowed in the form of tears, along with sweaty palms and shaky knees. I cried and told the counselor about the comments that had propelled me into the anger stage of grief. For the first time in my journey through this loss, I was provided words of wisdom that would begin to help mend my fractured soul.

She said, "It is better for people to say 'something' to you, even if it's upsetting, rather than to say nothing at all."

After she spoke, the counselor allowed the room to rest in silence as her words hung in the air. I mulled this statement over in my head.

Yes, of course. I would be far more hurt if those around us stayed away, or in conversation left our situation unacknowledged. I began to take solace in the thought that people cared enough about us to want to approach me, and to try to provide me with words that could possibly bring me comfort, even if in the end, those words had the opposite effect. There was absolutely nothing that anyone could have said that would have provided me with any relief from my pain. I wanted the pregnancy that Mother Nature took away from me, and there was nothing that could be done to reverse the outcome.

My husband and I left the counselor's office that day feeling as though a bit of weight had been lifted off of our shoulders. A few weeks later, I felt truly supported when someone said to me in very simple terms, "This is absolutely a shit situation. You have every right to feel shit, you have every right to talk shit, and it is totally normal if there is nothing on this planet that can be done to make you feel better until you have your healthy pregnancy."

I was finally given permission to feel sorry for myself. Guilt-free.

The healing continued to take place as I came across people who wanted to sit with me, allowed me to speak when I was ready, and let me say whatever I wanted to say at that moment, no matter how irrational. And when I became too exhausted to say any more, I was truly comforted when advice was withheld and we would sit comfortably in each other's presence, in the quiet and still of the room.

MY STORY

This is how my partner and I view counseling . . .

_____

_____

_____

_____

This is how our family and friends might react if they knew we were going to counseling . . .

_____

_____

_____

_____

_____

This is why I might/will/will not try counseling . . .

_____

_____

_____

_____

_____

_____

_____

_____

These are my expectations of counseling . . .

_____

_____

_____

_____

_____

_____

_____

_____

*"Many women . . . need to move past
the repetitive expression of their loss and to
plunge back into engagement with the living,
with projects, with all the things that may
supply meaning for their own lives."*

—IRVIN D. YALOM,
PSYCHOTHERAPIST AND AUTHOR

CHAPTER 13

Searching
for Meaning

After my first miscarriage, I really believed that
if I could just get pregnant a second time,
everything would be fine. I could move on with
life and leave all of the sadness that I had endured
behind me for good.

About a year after our devastating news, I
was sitting on my bed, alone in my room, when
an overwhelming feeling of calm came over me.
It felt as though someone was holding me tightly
and telling me that I could let go of my worry
and stress, that good news was in my near future.

It was a physical feeling of warmth, and in that moment, I felt my anxiety dissipate and my breathing slow and become steadier. The sun was shining brightly through the window, and I lifted my face toward the sun and shut my eyes. I remember smiling to myself and relishing the feeling of contentment in that moment. I then looked over at my bookshelves at the small, red Buddha figurine that one of my mother's friends had sent to me. He had a huge smile on his face and was holding an egg in each hand. Its owner had sworn that after rubbing the Buddha each day for a month, she had fallen pregnant after years of trying. I stood up and walked over to the tubby figure and rubbed its belly with my forefinger. I didn't really believe that this piece of ceramic had anything to do with whether or not I would conceive, but I didn't want to take any chances.

Two weeks later, I found out that I was pregnant, just as I thought I would be. The strong, supportive presence that I had felt in my bedroom that day truly left me believing that God or some higher power must be communicating with me, and when I got pregnant, this belief seemed to be confirmed.

So two weeks later when I miscarried for the second time, I was left feeling angry and confused. Was God toying with me? I had been in such a bad place, how could my mood have changed so drastically in that moment in my bedroom if it was not God? I couldn't grasp the unfairness of the situation. Hadn't I paid my dues? Hadn't I tried consistently for an entire year to get pregnant, only to have it taken away so quickly? I grabbed the Buddha—who in my mind had become a sentient being, sitting comfortably on my shelf, laughing at me—and I threw it into the trash can.

I would have to face this on my own.

I didn't feel the same degree of intense sadness that I did after the first miscarriage. Instead, my body began to defend itself with a shield of numbness. I went to my doctor to inform her of my second miscarriage and hoped that at this stage she might enact a plan of action for us to follow. After the first miscarriage, I was told to continue trying for a year to conceive, and if at that point I wasn't pregnant, we could discuss further options. It seemed that because I was able to become pregnant a second time, there was no real attempt to provide assistance. The "plumbing" was working, so there was no need for medical intervention. I would have to figure out when to try again, and because my menstrual cycles were still irregular, the thought of working to decipher when I was going to ovulate left me feeling exhausted, emotionally and physically. As I left the doctor's office, I tried to summon anger or sadness—any emotion at all. I just wanted to feel something, anything. But all I felt was empty.

Soon I was signing up for activities that I thought would fill the void that lived deep inside of my core. I began coaching a youth basketball team and taking piano lessons every Wednesday evening. I also signed up for a course in therapeutic counseling at the local community college. I had obtained a Master's Degree in counseling but had never taken the steps necessary to qualify as a practitioner, which I had always regretted. I decided that I would try to focus my energies on making up for lost time.

A couple of months after packing my schedule with activities, I realized that I liked the *ideas* of coaching and playing piano more than I actually enjoyed participating in those activities. I pulled back and decided to concentrate on my course, which was extremely challenging, yet therapeutic on many levels.

At the start of every class, sitting in a circle, each student would "check-in" to let everyone know where they were emotionally before starting our six-hour session for the day. Some days I would be the very last person to check in. I knew that as soon as I opened my mouth and began to speak, that sadness that I tried to contain in public would be pushed out in the open, naked and vulnerable. My thoughts and feelings would be available for anyone to scrutinize or rebuff. I also didn't want to hear the sadness in my own voice. I was often afraid that if the tears started, I wouldn't be able to stop the flow. I pictured my lecturers running around looking for wastebaskets to contain all my tears so that we wouldn't all be washed away.

My classmates had their own "stuff" they were struggling with, and I envied those who could disclose harrowing stories in front of the group without showing nearly such strong emotions. No chins quivering, voices breaking, and fingers rustling to find a tissue before makeup or a nose began to run. I often wondered how they were able to stay so calm.

Some nights before my class, I would think about what I was going to bring to check-in the next morning. I would envision myself speaking the truth, but doing so in a very matter-of-fact way with a straight face. I'd say my bit, and the class would continue without missing a beat. But the next day would roll around, and as soon as I'd check-in with the class and let the first few words out of my mouth, I'd feel my throat tightening and the tears pooling behind my eyes. I'd pause and try to gain my composure, but inevitably the tears would make their way to the surface. I would leave the class at break time feeling embarrassed and weak that I wasn't able to hold it together.

I spoke to my therapist (I was required to undergo 50 hours of therapy as part of the course) about my aim to act more like some of the others in my class. "They seem to have it together, despite the harrowing situations that they're dealing with," I said. My therapist tried to impress upon me that showing my emotions did not mean that I was weak, rather it meant that I was working through grief, instead of suppressing it. She felt that the others probably had a long way to go if they were not yet able to allow themselves to feel and express their emotions. As the course continued, I learned that she was quite right. Those who maintained a stiff upper lip didn't seem to be progressing and working through their issues, and eventually they would even admit to as much, and I became the one who was on the mend.

Finding an activity that I felt passionate about didn't erase my pain, but it caused a shift. Instead of feeling the heaviness pushing down on me from the top of my head down to my shoulders, the sadness began to spread its way around my body, making the weight easier to carry. Those emotions were still a part of me, but they were no longer controlling me. I just knew that I had to put something in place so that one day I could look back and know that something good, however small, had come out of these devastating experiences.

MY STORY

This is what I've done to try and cope with these
difficult times as best I can . . .

_____

_____

_____

_____

_____

_____

_____

This is what I have not yet done, but would like
to do, to help me through our situation . . .

_____

_____

_____

_____

_____

_____

_____

This is what may be stopping me from moving forward . . .

_____

_____

_____

_____

_____

_____

_____

This is what I'd like "moving forward" to look like for my partner and me . . .

_____

_____

_____

_____

_____

_____

_____

*"The greatest accomplishment
is not in never falling,
but in rising again
after you fall."*

—Vince Lombardi

CHAPTER 14

The Day I Found Myself Laughing

Partying and drinking with friends had slowed down leading up to my first pregnancy, as my life was headed into family mode. But when I realized that a baby wasn't in my near future, I had to channel my younger self to remember how to be a young woman living in London with relatively little responsibility. OK, I did have to pay a mortgage each month and show up for work every day, but I didn't have to take care of a life, and I found it hard to switch gears. I didn't care to go out to clubs or stay up all night drinking myself into a two-day hangover. I had had my days of partying, and as much fun as it all had been, I was ready for the next stage in life.

Oftentimes my husband and I would opt for a quiet night in. We started a tradition of opening a bottle of wine in the kitchen, slicing into a block of cheese, and sampling some olives. We would stand at the counter, enjoying the mix of flavors in our mouths, and we'd discuss our life plans. We would laugh, and sometimes we'd cry, but we made time for acknowledging and sharing our emotions with one another rather than hiding them away.

It was difficult discussing the future because we had no idea what was in store for us. How could we plan when we didn't know whether or not I would become pregnant in the near future? If I did conceive, would I carry the baby to full term or have another miscarriage? I was tired of my job and anxious to move on, but it didn't make sense to start afresh if a baby was in our near future. The university where I worked was only a few miles from our home, and they offered a decent maternity leave package. This was the place to be when starting a family. On the other hand, I feared that I was putting too much of my life on hold as we continued on our quest to conceive.

After one of our evenings of bonding, my husband and I retired to the sofa and started to watch a few recorded episodes of the TV show *Modern Family*. I don't remember the exact episode that we were watching, but I clearly remember the feeling I had when I heard myself start to laugh and how it felt when the muscles in my face flexed as I smiled from ear to ear. As I laughed, my body gently shook, and I continued to laugh long after the joke on the TV show was over.

In that moment, laughter was no longer a sort of involuntary reaction to something funny. Just as we aren't always conscious of our breathing, our need to inhale and exhale in order to survive, I had never thought about my laughter until now. It normally just . . . happened. But for the first time in my life, I had been startled by my own laughter, and I didn't want it to end. I was afraid of losing it again as I had over the past year. I wanted to bag it up and lock it away somewhere safe for those moments when I need it. Notice I said "need," not just "want." I need moments of laughter to remind me that I am still alive and that I will survive.

In your grief, when you have a moment of relief, a break from the pain, savor that time and remember just how sweet life can be. Let it fill you with life and reenergize your fatigued soul.

MY STORY

These are the poems/books/movies/TV shows/
quotes that have brought me comfort . . .

_____

_____

_____

_____

_____

_____

_____

_____

_____

_____

_____

_____

*"Biology is the least of
what makes someone a mother."*

—OPRAH WINFREY,
PHILANTHROPIST, PRODUCER, ACTRESS

CHAPTER 15

Is Adoption for Us?

After nearly three years of trying to conceive and maintain a healthy pregnancy, I was still hopeful that one day I would have my baby. My main frustration was that I had no idea when that day would be. If I had some sort of timeline that I could follow, I could put things in place to help me cope. But the not knowing of it all was draining. I began to think of ways that we could still move forward with our plans to become parents while we waited for my body to cooperate.

I decided to go online and begin looking into our options with regard to adoption. When I would discuss my findings with my husband, he would listen, but he did not respond further or ask me any questions. When I questioned him about his lack of engagement, his response was, "Adoption is an amazing thing and it takes such special people to go down that path. I'm not ruling it out, but I really want our first child to be biological. I really believe that it will happen for us." I responded by telling him that I agreed, that I had not given up on our chances of having a baby naturally either, but that I wanted to be a parent more than anything. So why not look into this in the meantime? I was afraid that five years would pass us by and we'd end up adopting after wasting years of our lives in limbo. In the end, my husband agreed to join me in attending a local adoption meeting to learn more.

My husband and I entered the meeting, which was held at the local town hall. It was a beautiful building with ornate woodwork and beautiful chandeliers, which didn't quite jive with the opened box of biscuits and cartons of juice that were ripped open and left on a table for us to help ourselves to. Couldn't they have at least put the biscuits out on a plate? It looked like someone just couldn't be bothered to make an effort, but I tried not to let the little things irritate me. The snack display should be the least of my worries.

We chose our seats in the first row, remembering how annoyed we felt when our students tried to cram themselves into the back row, as if the thought of learning anything at school filled them with absolute dread. I then began to look around the room to see what prospective adoptive parents look like. I don't know what I was imagining, but I was hoping I wouldn't see anyone that looked like Miss Hannigan from the movie *Annie*. The majority of couples looked to be in their forties or gay. We seemed to be the only heterosexual couple in our thirties. Once I pinpointed our differences, I began to wonder about our similarities. What had all of these people been through so far to try and become parents?

One pretty blonde woman had a bag of snacks that she nervously nibbled on as the presentation began. Any opportunity to ask a question and her hand would be the first to shoot up. Her questions were well planned and you could tell that she was not completely new to this process. Her husband sat quietly beside her, looking worn and weary, and my heart went out to both of them. Their desperation to start a family seemed to emanate around them.

The presenters from the local adoption agency had a PowerPoint, and they each took turns staring at the screen and reading off each piece of information word for word in monotone voices. It seemed like some sort of sketch from *Saturday Night Live,* and at one point I felt hysterical giggles coming on. Luckily, my husband shot me a keep-your-cool glance, and I got was able to pull it together and continue to listen.

We learned that there are few healthy newborns that are available for adoption, as the system works very hard to keep babies within the family, with the hopes of reintegrating the baby with the mother in time. Three- to five-year-olds are in greatest need of a home, and siblings are extremely hard to place in a loving family.

On our way out the door, there were magazines for us to take home that displayed siblings currently on their register and needing to leave their foster homes as soon as possible. It seemed so strange, browsing a magazine to pick out a child, just as you would a new pair of winter boots. I was able to read between the lines when looking at the descriptions of the children and to determine which kids had quite severe emotional problems.

Later when discussing our experience and the magazine with some of our acquaintances, someone made the comment, "Oh yeah, you have to be careful about not adopting a child that has a lot of problems . . ." Another said, "You wouldn't want to bring a troubled child into your home." These comments sickened me. Someone has to love and care for these children. It's not their fault that they were brought into unstable homes and are now acting out as a consequence! How dare we turn our back on these children! As my husband and I discussed some of these less-than-acceptable reactions, he agreed with my response but still did not feel that he was ready to adopt at this point in our lives. I felt saddened but knew that we absolutely could not move forward unless we both felt that the time was right. It would be a huge undertaking and an extremely challenging one at that, so this pathway to parenthood would have to be put on hold for the time being.

MY STORY

These are my feelings with regard to adoption . . .

_____

_____

_____

_____

_____

_____

_____

_____

These are my partner's feelings around adoption . . .

_____

_____

_____

_____

_____

_____

_____

_____

We feel the way we do about adoption
because . . .

_____

_____

_____

_____

_____

_____

_____

_____

*"If you're going through hell,
keep going."*

—WINSTON CHURCHILL

CHAPTER 16

Strike Three

Halfway through my counseling course, I had a third miscarriage. This one hurt less than the last. It was quick. The day after I had a positive pregnancy test, I began to bleed. I was on holiday with my husband at one of our favorite places on the planet, the island of Cyprus. I left my sun lounger and the cool shade of our bright blue umbrella to trek through the piping hot sand to the nearest toilet. When I made it into the stuffy stall and pulled down my bathing suit bottoms, I saw a dark brown streak of blood and my heart sank. *Not again.*

I walked back to my husband, avoiding parents and babies along the way. As always, he greeted me with a smile and immediately knew that something was wrong. "I'm bleeding," I said, biting my lower lip and trying not to cry. We spent the next hour in silence, staring out at the beautiful turquoise waves crashing against the white sands. I felt exhausted—too tired to expend any energy talking about our latest loss. Besides, what was left to say? We had been here before, and it was more than clear that we were just not in control over this part of our lives.

Never one to drown my sorrows with alcohol, I was suddenly craving a stiff drink. We left the beach and headed back to our flat. When we arrived, my husband and I poured ourselves a brandy and lemonade. I lit a Vogue cigarette and turned on the music of one of our favorite bands. We barely spoke, but we didn't need to. We each knew what the other was thinking and feeling, and it was enough to just sit closely in each other's presence. Of course, I was upset. But there was a strength that I hadn't felt before that was keeping me from going back to that dark place that I had fallen into after the first miscarriage. I wouldn't let this ruin our trip. We needed this holiday.

I also began to feel that with each miscarriage, we just had to be that much closer to our happy ending. Maybe I was wrong, but I had to hold onto that glimmer of hope that I felt rising inside of me.

When we arrived back in the UK after our trip, I immediately got in touch with my doctor. I wanted her to know that I was starting my third year of trying to conceive and maintain a healthy pregnancy and that there must be more tests or treatment that we were eligible for at this stage. At one point, a doctor had said that I might have polycystic ovaries, but nothing was ever mentioned of this again. I became increasingly driven to find out if there was some simple solution to my body's struggle that perhaps was just being overlooked.

My husband and I had already visited the Sub-Fertility Unit at our hospital three times, and we were not happy with the responses that we received from the doctors. One male doctor who appeared to be in his early 70s explained to me in a very condescending tone of voice how the reproductive system works. At another appointment, a middle-aged female doctor's answer was for me to just relax and start drinking more wine. They also provided me with timelines that were never adhered to. For example, one doctor told me that I had to try for at least a year before they would help me. A year rolled around, and suddenly the timeline changed to two years. When I had my third miscarriage and started my third year of trying to conceive again, I wrote the hospital a letter outlining our frustrations over our lack of support. Finally, we received the response we had been waiting to hear.

The head of the Sub-Fertility Unit wrote me a very kind letter, acknowledging my frustrations and requesting that we discuss the situation further in person rather than in writing. About a month later, my husband and I were back at the hospital waiting eagerly to meet this doctor. In she came to the medical room with her red streaks of dyed curly hair. She was kind and gentle and immediately put us at ease. Without defending her fellow doctors, she said that patients should never leave their doctor's appointment feeling worse than when they came in. She explained what might have been preventing a healthy pregnancy, and proposed a specific plan for moving forward.

It was amazing how well she was able to empathize with our situation. Half the time, she took the words right out of our mouths. We were astonished and left the appointment feeling great, and a few weeks later, my husband and I were scheduled to begin Intrauterine Insemination (IUI).

MY STORY

This is what my partner and I have done or would like to do to serve as strong advocates for ourselves . . .

_____

_____

_____

_____

_____

_____

_____

The doctors have provided us a treatment plan that is . . .

_____

_____

_____

_____

_____

_____

_____

Having this plan in place makes me feel . . .

_____

_____

_____

_____

_____

_____

_____

_____

_____

"Never give up on something that
you can't go a day without thinking about."
—AMERICA ADOPTS!

CHAPTER 17

Treatment

I have read that some women feel quite discouraged if they have to resort to fertility treatment to assist with conception. Don't we all prefer it when things work out naturally? But by this point, I had given up on my husband and I making progress on our own, and I was ecstatic to be receiving assistance.

We met with an older Asian doctor in the Sub-Fertility Unit. She was extremely kind, but even more, she was fiercely focused on her task: getting me pregnant. The first stage of the treatment process consisted of me taking a pill called Clomiphene, which is used to stimulate ovulation.

I would take this from day 2 through 6 of my next cycle. Then on days 10, 12, and 14 I would travel to the hospital for internal scans so that they could monitor the follicles' reaction to the pill. When the follicle(s) grew to the appropriate size, I would then be given an injection in my backside to encourage the follicle(s) to release the egg(s). In my case, only one follicle was at the correct size at my scan on day 14. So the very next day, I returned to the hospital for my injection. Paul was shown how to do it himself in case I needed further treatment cycles that might involve daily injections. It saddened me to think of things getting to that point, but I tried to focus on the task at hand.

The day after the injection, I had to report to a hospital in central London with my husband in tow in order for him to produce a sperm sample. The sample was prepared in a solution, isolating the most motile sperm into one sample, and we were then sent back to our local hospital for the insemination.

The doctor had told us that most women respond to the treatment on the second cycle. I couldn't imagine going through this process more than once and prayed that this time we would be lucky and things would work out right away. Only time would tell.

On the day that my husband had to give his

sperm sample, we pulled up to the old Victorian hospital, which looked ominous under the dark clouds that loomed above. My husband was unusually quiet, and we wandered around the hospital grounds trying to find the correct building. We needed area C, but of course could only find A, B, D, E, and F. We finely found another human, a friendly member of staff, who pointed us in the right direction. When we arrived at the lab, there was already a line of couples waiting outside. I didn't know whether we should engage with the others and make some sort of a crude joke to take the pressure off or keep our heads down.

Everyone kept their eyes to the floor. We did the same.

About 15 minutes later, the lab door opened, and a man with a long, white trench coat and gray-colored skin and hair that seemed to blend into one was there to greet us. I felt as if we were entering the Addams Family home. He seemed more like a cartoon character, and I felt as though I were in some sort of a dream. I leaned over to my husband. "Why does the man who deals with the sperm have to look so creepy? I bet he has cameras hooked up in all of the rooms." My husband smiled at me and rolled his eyes as he picked up a clipboard and began filling in the details.

Two hours later, we were back in the car and driving to our local hospital for the insemination. I chuckled to myself, proud of my husband for completing his task faster than the other men in the room. I was anxious to get back to the hospital, as if there were only a set number of women who could have the procedure done and I needed to get there first. Of course that was nonsense, but I had this feeling of competitiveness running through me.

When we arrived at the hospital, I was shown to a room and asked to strip off my bottoms and get onto the bed. My husband handed the nurse the sperm sample, and she put it into a syringe to prepare for the injection. I lay on the bed thinking about my loss of inhibition around having my lady bits on show so regularly these days. I wanted to open the door and shout down the hallway, "Anyone else want to come take a look while I'm here?"

The procedure was quick and consisted of the sperm being inserted high up into my uterus where, fingers crossed, one of the little guys would fertilize my egg. When the nurse was done with her part, she asked me to curl my legs over to the side and lay there for about 20 minutes before I could leave. When she exited the room, my husband and I sat there looking at each other and wondering how our bodies ever let us get to this point.

MY STORY

These are our feelings around the prospect of treatment or our feelings since we've started treatment . . .

_____

_____

_____

_____

_____

_____

_____

This is how we have coped with the multiple hospital appointments, medications and more . . .

_____

_____

_____

_____

_____

_____

_____

Our employers were/weren't supportive of our time
needed out of the office for treatment . . .

_____

_____

_____

_____

_____

_____

_____

_____

"I am half agony, half hope."

—JANE AUSTEN, NOVELIST

CHAPTER 18

The Results Are In

As expected, the two-week wait between the insemination and the day that I could take a pregnancy test felt agonizingly long. I had booked a trip to San Diego, California, to visit my younger brother who had recently lost his partner in a tragic car accident. I felt that I needed to get out to see him again, but I also didn't want anything to get in the way of treatment. In the end, I managed to juggle both important activities. I arrived in the States on a Wednesday, and on that Friday I would be able to take the pregnancy test.

I was hyper-aware of every change my body was making. My abdomen was significantly bloated, and my breasts were sore. I was afraid to believe that this could be the result of a pregnancy and began making excuses for the changes. *Maybe these symptoms occur from this type of treatment,* I would say to myself. I was hesitant to read too much online, as I realized that there are a lot of women who have a baby and suddenly think they are the experts on all reproductive matters.

The big day finally arrived, and as soon as I woke up that morning, I took a pregnancy test. Stupidly, I bought one of the cheapest tests that showed either one pink line or two. My test result showed one solid line in the test window and a mostly faded second pink line in the other.

That result wasn't good enough. I kept thinking that my eyes were deceiving me and that the faded pink line was just in my imagination. So later that day, I bought a $20 test that would either say "Pregnant" or "Not Pregnant" in the little window. Since I wanted to use my first urine of the day, I kept a little piece of hope in my heart and managed to carry on with my Friday in relative calm.

The next morning, the pricey test confirmed my result—"Pregnant 2–3 weeks." This was totally accurate given the time since the insemination.

I sent my husband back in the UK a picture of

the test and waited for his reply. He called me right away, and although we were both incredibly excited, a hesitancy to open ourselves up to such happiness remained. We knew that our journey was far from over and that we had to be prepared for anything to happen over the next three months. I dreamed of the day when I would finally be entering into my second trimester and would hopefully be able to feel more confident that everything would be all right.

Our families were absolutely thrilled to hear our news, but at the same time, they acted with caution, which we appreciated. They didn't ask questions about things happening too far into the future as they knew that we weren't going to assume that everything would work out from that point forward.

As the weeks continued, family and friends would send me text messages each Friday when I'd enter a new week of the first trimester. "Yay! You're nearing week eight! Hang in there! Don't forget to let me know when your next doctor's appointment will be!" The steady flow of communication reminded me that we are loved and that there are a lot of people rooting for us. And although no one could take away my worries completely, I was able to recognize that no matter what happened, I wouldn't have to face it alone.

Three times during the first trimester I had what was called "implantation bleeding." I had thought that this only happened very early on, when the egg would first implant itself into the uterine wall. However, a doctor told me that implantation bleeding can occur throughout the first trimester. The first time the bleeding occurred, I was hiking with my husband in Wales. I went to the toilet only to find a dark brown spot of blood in my underwear. I let out a sharp breath, my chest deflated, and I sat frozen on the toilet. *No, this cannot happen again.*

I finally got myself out of the bathroom and gave my husband that look that he had seen several times before. "Are you all right?" he asked. I told him what I had found, and we began to hike our way back to our accommodation in silence. There was only a tiny bit of blood after that, but I had myself convinced that this was the start of a miscarriage. When we returned home the next day, we called the hospital, and they immediately invited us in for an early scan. I kept telling my husband that we should prepare ourselves to not see a heartbeat like we had seen at 6.5 weeks when the doctor at the Sub-Fertility Unite confirmed the pregnancy.

But we were lucky that day, as we were the next two times after that when I had further bleeding. At each scan, I was told that they did not see anything wrong and that bleeding can occur for many reasons, some unexplained. My initial reaction was to once again curse God and ask him why anything having to do with pregnancy can't run smoothly for me?! But instead, I decided to think of myself as one of the lucky ones. I was able to see the growth of the embryo-turned-fetus three times before my 12-week scan, when most women would be getting only their first glimpse of their growing baby. Even when we only saw a blob that looked more like a hamster than anything else, we were in awe. As soon as the scan technician would point out the heartbeat, my husband and I would feel a bit of tension lift from our shoulders, and we'd both stare at the monitor with smiles plastered across our faces.

From that day forward, friends, family, and colleagues would continue to check in with me on how the pregnancy was progressing. I was very careful not to say too much around people that I wasn't familiar with. I didn't want to talk excitedly about my pregnancy if I was in the company of someone who might be struggling themselves. I told my manager that I didn't want any sort of announcement made for me at work, that if I were so lucky to carry this baby to full term, people would naturally find out through seeing my changing figure.

Not only did I not want to inadvertently upset anyone, but also I was afraid that if I let myself really believe that this pregnancy would make it to full term, I might jinx myself. My friends and my counselor all tried to reassure me that there was no such thing as a jinx and that I should allow myself to bask in the miracle at hand. I so badly wanted to trust them, to begin letting go of all of the sadness I had felt such a short time ago, but it was hard. For the entire first trimester, every time I went to the bathroom, I dreaded what I might see. Would there be blood? If so, how much? Sometimes I would try pretending that this was my first ever pregnancy and that I was naïve to thoughts that anything could go wrong. And for that split second, I could actually feel unadulterated joy.

MY STORY

This is our success story, or this is what we hope
our story will one day be . . .

_____

_____

_____

_____

_____

_____

_____

_____

_____

_____

_____

_____

_____

_____

_____

_____

_____

_____

*"I wanted you to see something about her—
I wanted you to see what real courage is . . .
It's when you know you're licked before
you begin, but you begin anyway
and you see it through, no matter what.
You rarely win, but sometimes you do."*

—ATTICUS FINCH, *TO KILL A MOCKINGBIRD*
BY HARPER LEE

CHAPTER 19

A Different Kind of Ending

As I finish this book, I am still pregnant. I do not know what the outcome of my story will be, but amidst the ever-present worry, I must hold on to that sliver of hope that everything will be OK. I'm not sure what "OK" will look like, but I hope that the yearning will fade and that I will feel happiness and contentment, whether that includes a baby in my future or not. I want my relationship with my husband to stay strong because we couldn't have weathered the stormy times together for nothing. I want my life to feel purposeful and full of meaning. This time around, I want a different kind of ending.

But to be honest, if this pregnancy ceases to continue at any point, I don't know how I will react or what my future plans will be. As much as I want to start a family, I don't know how many cycles of treatment I can endure. I hear the truly amazing success stories about the number of years and treatment cycles that other women have gone through to finally have a baby. I just don't know if I have the endurance to go where others have gone.

And I think that's OK, too.

When I hear about women who are childless because of infertility, I also look at them in awe. So many of these women have continued leading fulfilling lives, and many are making a difference in this world even though they have had every excuse to feel bitter and withdraw from a place that can feel so unfair—so ugly.

My final word to you is that YOU ARE STRONG. I have found that even when we feel the weakest, we're actually at our strongest, because it takes real strength to pull ourselves out from the depths of the sadness and grief that stems from loss. When you cannot seem to find your strength, I hope that you can pick up this book and be reminded of all the circumstances you have already made it through and know that you will be OK.

*"Sooner or later, you have to give up
the hope for a better past."*

—IRVIN D. YALOM,
PSYCHOTHERAPIST AND AUTHOR

The Show Must Go On

If you are still working toward conceiving and maintaining a healthy pregnancy, please remember that this is a time for you to be selfish and to focus on just you and your partner. If that means avoiding Christmas with your family because you can't bear being around your siblings and their babbling babies, then so be it. Now is not the time to worry about what others may be thinking of your actions.

Please take heed: Do what YOU need to do in the name of healing.

At the same time, the show must go on. We must continue facing this world of proud parents and beautiful babies. We will most likely hear of a handful or more of our friends getting pregnant . . . on their first try . . . after just coming off of birth control . . . which they had been taking for at least the past decade. We may have to bear witness to people's happiness, while silently falling apart on the inside. There is nowhere to hide. Everyone has struggles in life, and this one is ours.

I have accepted that all I can do is strive to maintain a feeling of positivity as much as I can but accept that there will be times when this is just near impossible. I am trying to accept that I will have more days of feeling at my absolute lowest and wondering how much more sadness I can take before it kills me. But I will soldier on, because the only other option is to lie down and let the world pass me by. One day, although I can't say when, I must continue to hope that I will feel all of the joy that life can afford once again.

I'd like to think that women's experiences of miscarrying or infertility, if discussed more, will help other couples as they traverse this rocky path to parenthood. I hope that the sharing of our stories will better inform family and friends of how to support loved ones who have lost a pregnancy, because I want our situation to be understood.

For a moment, we had one of the greatest of loves, a love that is shared between a mother and a baby, but it was taken away from us sooner than it should have been. This love is fierce and rages inside of us. Take that away, and we are broken. But there is hope, and there is healing. And in time, we will feel this love again, this love that so many take for granted.

"Whatever teaches us to talk to ourselves is important: whatever teaches us to sing ourselves out of despair."
—THEODORE DECKER,
THE GOLDFINCH BY DONNA TARTT

About the Author

Jaclyn Pieris currently works in the field of Student Affairs in higher education and is a certified therapeutic counselor. Originally from Pennsylvania, she and her British-born husband live in London, England, with their newborn baby boy.